The Noble Qur'an

Hizb Al'ala

حزب الأعلى

Arabic-English
Phonetic Transliteration

Learn how to pronounce Arabic alphabets

Letter	"Name"	Pronunciation	Transliteration
ا	"alif"	"a" as in "bat," but elongated if in middle/at end of word (not elongated if at beginning of word); may be long vowel	a, ā
ب	"ba"	"b" as in "boy"	b
ت	"ta"	"t" as in "tap"	t
ث	"tha"	unvoiced "th" as in "three"	th
ج	"jeem"	"j" as in "jump" (Egyptian colloquial: hard "g" as in "grab")	j
ح	"haa"	similar to an English "h" but very pronounced and very raspy	h
خ	"kha"	sounds like the German "ch" in "ich" or the "kh" in "shaykh" (this latter example is technically cheating since it is an Arabic word)	kh
د	"dal"	"d" as in "day"	d
ذ	"dhal"	voiced "th" as in "that"	dh
ر	"ra"	"r" as in "run"	r
ز	"za"	"z" as in "zebra"	z
س	"seen"	"s" as in, er, "seen"	s
ش	"sheen"	"sh" as in, um, "sheen"	sh
ص	"saad"	"emphatic" or "pharyngealized" (said with a constricted pharynx or epiglottis)"s"	ş
ض	"daad"	"emphatic" or "pharyngealized" "d"	đ
ط	"taa"	"emphatic" or "pharyngealized" "t"	ţ
ظ	"zaa"	"emphatic" or "pharyngealized" "dh" or "z" (pronunciation varies)	
ع	"ayn"	the most unusual sound in the Arabic alphabet for an English speaker; like "a" in "tab" but as if you were choking	', '
غ	"ghayn"	classically pronounced like "r" in French or German, but regionally may sound like a soft "g" as in the Greek "gyro" or like a hard English "g" (particularly when used in loanwords)	gh
ف	"fa"	"f" as in "far"	f
ق	"qaf"	regional pronunciation varies from hard "g" to "k," but classically really sounds like a "q" if you can separate the "q" sound from the "u" that always follows in in English, or like the "q" in the French "quatre"	q
ك	"kaf"	"k" as in "king"	k
ل	"lam"	"l" as in "lamb"	l
م	"meem"	"m" as in "mark"	m
ن	"noon"	"n" as in, well, "noon"	n
ه	"ha"	"h" as in "has"	h

و	"waw"	as in "way" or "u"/"oo" as in "pool" or "rune"; may be long vowel	w
ي	"ya"	"y" as in "yellow" or long "e"/"i" as in "me"; may be long vowel	y

Non-Alphabetic Characters

Letter	"Name"	Pronunciation	Transliteration
◌َ	"fatha" (fat-ha)	short vowel "a" as in "bat"	a
◌ِ	"kasra"	short vowel "i" as in "bit"	i
◌ُ	"damma"	short vowel "u" as in "put"	u
◌ّ	"shadda"	signifies a doubling/lengthening of the consonant on which it sits	doubled consonant
◌ْ	"sukoon"	signifies the absence of any short vowel, very rarely used and will be very rarely used here	N/A
ة	"ta marbuta"	feminine marker found only at end of word, adds an "-a" sound	-a, -ah, -at
ى	"alif maqsura"	identical to "long a" alif, alternate form sometimes found at end of word	-á
ء	"hamza"	glottal stop, like the short break in the middle of "uh-oh"; usually attached to a "seat" in the form of one of the long vowel characters, like أ ؤ ئ, in which case it turns the long vowel it's sitting on into a short vowel with a stop	', '

Transcription System

ā á Ā	long "a" like a in the word (palm)
u	like "ou / o"
ū	like a long "u" (like "u" in the word "assume")
ī	long "i" (like "ie" in the word achieve)
Gh	like "r" in frensh , (Pronounced as the Parisian R)
Th	like "th" in the word (Three)
Dh	like "th" in the word (Mother)
ž Ž	Like "dh" but the bottom of the tongue moves towards the throat, the vowel that will follow will be more serious and magnified
Sh	like "ch" in the word (Shy)
Kh	Like "kh" in the name (Kkhalid)
R r	like "r" spanish
`	Pronounce "a" from the back of the throat as in the Arabic word (`li)
Q q	Make "k" but with the bottom of the tongue towards the tongue towards the throat as for the mouth, you will feel its get out of this place.
T t	like "t"
ţ Ţ	like "t" in the word "Tom" (T Guttural)
D d	like "d"
đ Đ	like "D" in the word "Donald" (D Guttural)
S s	like "s" in the word "sick"
Ş ş	like "s" in the word "son" (S Guttural)
ĥ Ĥ	like "H" in the word (Hamza)

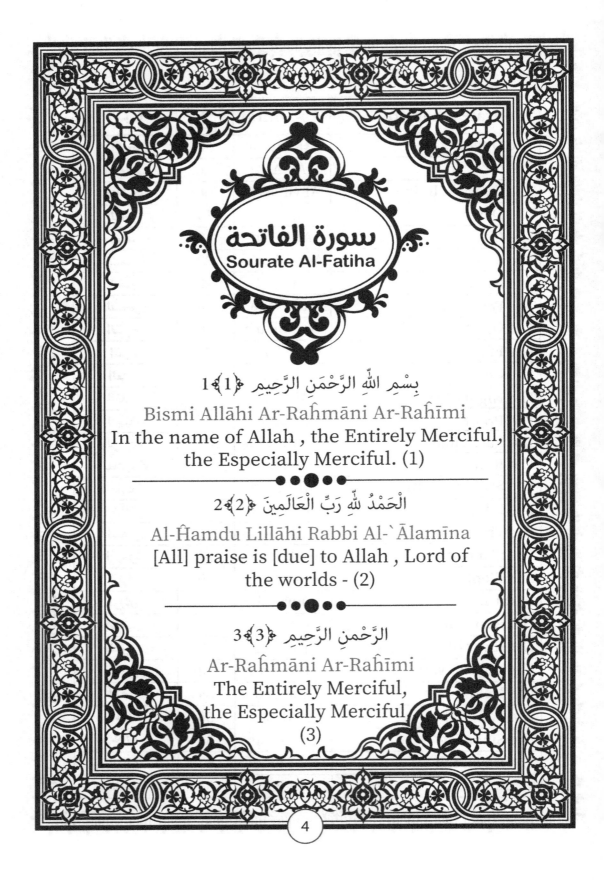

سورة الفاتحة
Sourate Al-Fatiha

بِسْمِ اللَّهِ الرَّحْمَنِ الرَّحِيمِ ﴿1﴾ 1

Bismi Allāhi Ar-Raḥmāni Ar-Raḥīmi
In the name of Allah , the Entirely Merciful,
the Especially Merciful. (1)

الْحَمْدُ للَّهِ رَبِّ الْعَالَمِينَ ﴿2﴾ 2

Al-Ĥamdu Lillāhi Rabbi Al-`Ālamīna
[All] praise is [due] to Allah , Lord of
the worlds - (2)

الرَّحْمَنِ الرَّحِيمِ ﴿3﴾ 3

Ar-Raḥmāni Ar-Raḥīmi
The Entirely Merciful,
the Especially Merciful
(3)

مَلِكِ يَوْمِ الدِّينِ ﴿4﴾ 4

Māliki Yawmi Ad-Dīni
Sovereign of the Day of Recompense. (4)

•••••

إِيَّاكَ نَعْبُدُ وَإِيَّاكَ نَسْتَعِينُ ﴿5﴾ 5

'Īyāka Na`budu Wa 'Īyāka Nasta`īnu
It is You we worship and You we
ask for help.(5)

•••••

اهدِنَا الصِّرَاطَ المُستَقِيمَ ﴿6﴾ 6

Ihdinā Aş-Şirāţa Al-Mustaqīma
Guide us to the straight path - (6)

•••••

صِرَاطَ الَّذِينَ أنعَمتَ
عَلَيهِمْ غَيرِ المَغضُوبِ عَلَيهِمْ وَلاَ الضَّالِّينَ ﴿7﴾ 7

Şirāţa Al-Ladhīna 'An`amta `Alayhim Ghayri
Al-Maghđūbi `Alayhim Wa Lā Ađ-Đāllīna

The path of those upon whom You have be-
stowed favor, not of those who have evoked
[Your] anger or of those who are astray.

Bismi Allāhi Ar-Raḥmāni Ar-Raḥīmi بِسْمِ اللهِ الرَّحْمَٰنِ الرَّحِيمِ

سَبِّحِ اسْمَ رَبِّكَ الْأَعْلَى ﴿1﴾ 1

Sabbiḥi isma Rabbika Al-'A`lá

Exalt the name of your Lord, the Most High, (1)

الَّذِي خَلَقَ فَسَوَّى ﴿2﴾ 2

Al-Ladhī Khalaqa Fasawwá

Who created and proportioned(2)

وَالَّذِي قَدَّرَ فَهَدَى ﴿3﴾ 3

Wa Al-Ladhī Qaddara Fahadá

And Who destined and [then] guided (3)

وَالَّذِي أَخْرَجَ الْمَرْعَى ﴿4﴾ 4

Wa Al-Ladhī 'Akhraja Al-Mar`á

And who brings out the pasture (4)

فَجَعَلَهُ غُثَاء أَحْوَى ﴿5﴾ 5

Faja`alahu Ghuthā'an 'Aḥwá

And [then] makes it black stubble. (5)

سَنُقْرِؤُكَ فَلَا تَنسَى ﴾6﴿ 6

Sanuqri'uka Falā Tansá
We will make you recite, [O Muhammad],
and you will not forget, (6)

─────────────●●●●●─────────────

إِلَّا مَا شَاءَ اللَّهُ إِنَّهُ يَعْلَمُ الْجَهْرَ وَمَا يَخْفَى ﴾7﴿ 7

'Illā Mā Shā'a Allāhu
'Innahu Ya`lamu Al-Jahra Wa Mā Yakhfá
Except what Allah should will. Indeed, He knows
what is declared and what is hidden.
(7)

─────────────●●●●●─────────────

وَنُيَسِّرُكَ لِلْيُسْرَى ﴾8﴿ 8

Wa Nuyassiruka Lilyusrá
And We will ease you toward ease.(8)

─────────────●●●●●─────────────

فَذَكِّرْ إِن نَّفَعَتِ الذِّكْرَى ﴾9﴿ 9

Fadhakkir 'In Nafa`ati Adh-Dhikrá
So remind, if the reminder should benefit; (9)

─────────────●●●●●─────────────

سَيَذَّكَّرُ مَن يَخْشَى ﴾10﴿ 10

Sayadhakkaru Man Yakhshá
He who fears [Allah] will be reminded.(10)

وَيَتَجَنَّبُهَا الْأَشْقَى ﴿11﴾ 11

Wa Yatajannabuhā Al-'Ashqá
But the wretched one will avoid it - (11)

• • • •

الَّذِي يَصْلَى النَّارَ الْكُبْرَى ﴿12﴾ 12

Al-Ladhī Yaşlá An-Nāra Al-Kubrá
[He] who will [enter and] burn in the greatest Fire, (12)

• • • •

ثُمَّ لَا يَمُوتُ فِيهَا وَلَا يَحْيَى ﴿13﴾ 13

Thumma Lā Yamūtu Fīhā Wa Lā Yaĥyā
Neither dying therein nor living. (13)

• • • •

قَدْ أَفْلَحَ مَن تَزَكَّى ﴿14﴾ 14

Qad 'Aflaĥa Man Tazakká
He has certainly succeeded who purifies himself (14)

• • • •

وَذَكَرَ اسْمَ رَبِّهِ فَصَلَّى ﴿15﴾ 15

Wa Dhakara Asma Rabbihi Faşallá
And mentions the name of his Lord and prays. (15)

• • • •

بَلْ تُؤْثِرُونَ الْحَيَاةَ الدُّنْيَا ﴿16﴾ 16

Bal Tu'uthirūna Al-Ĥayāata Ad-Dunyā
But you prefer the worldly life, (16)

وَالْآخِرَةُ خَيْرٌ وَأَبْقَى ﴿17﴾ 17

Wa Al-'Ākhiratu Khayrun Wa 'Abqá

While the Hereafter is better and more
enduring.(17)

• • • • •

إِنَّ هَذَا لَفِي الصُّحُفِ الْأُولَى ﴿18﴾ 18

'Inna Hādhā Lafī Aş-Şuĥufi Al-'Ūlá

Indeed, this is in the former scriptures,(18)

• • • •

صُحُفِ إِبْرَاهِيمَ وَمُوسَى ﴿19﴾ 19

Şuĥufi 'Ibrāhīma Wa Mūsá

The scriptures of Abraham and Moses.(19)

سورة الْغَاشِيَة
Sourate Al-Ghashiya

Bismi Allāhi Ar-Raĥmāni Ar-Raĥīmi بِسْمِ اللَّهِ الرَّحْمَنِ الرَّحِيمِ

هَلْ أَتَاكَ حَدِيثُ الْغَاشِيَةِ ﴿1﴾ 1

Hal 'Atāka Ĥadīthu Al-Ghāshiyati

Has there reached you the report of th
Overwhelming [event]? (1)

• • • • •

وُجُوهٌ يَوْمَئِذٍ خَاشِعَةٌ ﴿2﴾ 2

Wujūhun Yawma'idhin Khāshi`atun

[Some] faces, that Day, will be humbled,(2)

عَامِلَةٌ نَّاصِبَةٌ ﴿3﴾ 3

`Āmilatun Nāşibatun

Working [hard] and exhausted. (3)

• • • • •

تَصْلَى نَارًا حَامِيَةً ﴿4﴾ 4

Taşlá Nārāan Ĥāmiyatan

They will [enter to] burn in an intensely hot Fire. (4)

• • • • •

تُسْقَى مِنْ عَيْنٍ آنِيَةٍ ﴿5﴾ 5

Tusqá Min `Aynin 'Āniyatin

They will be given drink from a boiling spring. (5)

• • • • •

لَّيْسَ لَهُمْ طَعَامٌ إِلَّا مِن ضَرِيعٍ ﴿6﴾ 6

Laysa Lahum Ţa`āmun 'Illā Min Đarī`in

For them there will be no food except from
a poisonous, thorny plant(6)

• • • • •

لَا يُسْمِنُ وَلَا يُغْنِي مِن جُوعٍ ﴿7﴾ 7

Lā Yusminu Wa Lā Yughnī Min Jū`in

Which neither nourishes nor avails against hunger.(7)

• • • • •

وُجُوهٌ يَوْمَئِذٍ نَّاعِمَةٌ ﴿8﴾ 8

Wujūhun Yawma'idhin Nā`imatun

[Other] faces, that Day, will show pleasure. (8)

لِسَعْيِهَا رَاضِيَةٌ ﴿9﴾ 9

Lisa`yihā Rāđiyatun

With their effort [they are] satisfied (9)

•••••

فِي جَنَّةٍ عَالِيَةٍ ﴿10﴾ 10

Fī Jannatin `Āliyatin

In an elevated garden, (10)

•••••

لَّا تَسْمَعُ فِيهَا لَاغِيَةً ﴿11﴾ 11

Lā Tasma`u Fīhā Lāghiyatan

Wherein they will hear no unsuitable speech. (11)

•••••

فِيهَا عَيْنٌ جَارِيَةٌ ﴿12﴾ 12

Fīhā `Aynun Jāriyatun

Within it is a flowing spring. (12)

•••••

فِيهَا سُرُرٌ مَّرْفُوعَةٌ ﴿13﴾ 13

Fīhā Sururun Marfū`atun

Within it are couches raised high (13)

•••••

وَأَكْوَابٌ مَّوْضُوعَةٌ ﴿14﴾ 14

Wa 'Akwābun Mawđū`atun

And cups put in place (14)

وَنَمَارِقُ مَصْفُوفَةٌ ﴿15﴾ 15

Wa Namāriqu Maṣfūfatun
And cushions lined up (15)

• • • • •

وَزَرَابِيُّ مَبْثُوثَةٌ ﴿16﴾ 16

Wa Zarābīyu Mabthūthatun
And carpets spread around. (16)

• • • • •

أَفَلَا يَنظُرُونَ إِلَى الْإِبِلِ كَيْفَ خُلِقَتْ ﴿17﴾ 17

'Afalā Yanẓurūna 'Ilá Al-'Ibili Kayfa Khuliqat.
Then do they not look at the camels -
how they are created?(17)

• • • • •

وَإِلَى السَّمَاء كَيْفَ رُفِعَتْ ﴿18﴾ 18

Wa 'Ilá As-Samā'i Kayfa Rufi`at.
And at the sky - how it is raised?(18)

• • • • •

وَإِلَى الْجِبَالِ كَيْفَ نُصِبَتْ ﴿19﴾ 19

Wa 'Ilá Al-Jibāli Kayfa Nuṣibat
And at the mountains - how they are erected? (19)

• • • • •

وَإِلَى الْأَرْضِ كَيْفَ سُطِحَتْ ﴿20﴾ 20

Wa 'Ilá Al-'Arđi Kayfa Suṭiḥat
And at the earth - how it is spread out?(20)

فَذَكِّرْ إِنَّمَا أَنتَ مُذَكِّرٌ ﴿21﴾ 21

Fa dhakkir 'Innamā 'Anta Mudhakkirun.
So remind, [O Muhammad]; you are only
a reminder. (21)

• • • •

لَّسْتَ عَلَيْهِم بِمُصَيْطِرٍ ﴿22﴾ 22

Lasta `Alayhim Bimusayṭirin
You are not over them a controller. (22)

• • • •

إِلَّا مَن تَوَلَّى وَكَفَرَ ﴿23﴾ 23

Illā Man Tawallá Wa Kafara
However, he who turns away and disbelieves -(23)

• • • •

فَيُعَذِّبُهُ اللَّهُ الْعَذَابَ الْأَكْبَرَ ﴿24﴾ 24

Fayu`adhibuhu Allāhu Al-`Adhāba Al-'Akbara
Then Allah will punish him with the greatest
punishment.(24)

• • • •

إِنَّ إِلَيْنَا إِيَابَهُمْ ﴿25﴾ 25

Inna 'Ilaynā iyābahum
Indeed, to Us is their return. (25)

• • • •

ثُمَّ إِنَّ عَلَيْنَا حِسَابَهُمْ ﴿26﴾ 26

Thumma 'Inna `Alaynā Ĥisābahum
Then indeed, upon Us is their account.(26)

Bismi Allāhi Ar-Raḥmāni Ar-Raḥīmi
بِسْمِ اللهِ الرَّحْمَٰنِ الرَّحِيمِ

وَالْفَجْرِ ﴿1﴾ 1

Wa Al-Fajri
By the dawn (1)

● ● ● ● ●

وَلَيَالٍ عَشْرٍ ﴿2﴾ 2

Wa Layālin `Ashrin.
And [by] ten nights (2)

● ● ● ● ●

وَالشَّفْعِ وَالْوَتْرِ ﴿3﴾ 3

Wa Ash-Shaf`i Wa Al-Watri
And [by] the even [number] and the odd(3)

● ● ● ● ●

وَاللَّيْلِ إِذَا يَسْرِ ﴿4﴾ 4

Wa Al-Layli 'Idhā Yasri
And [by] the night when it passes,(4)

● ● ● ● ●

هَلْ فِي ذَٰلِكَ قَسَمٌ لِّذِي حِجْرٍ ﴿5﴾ 5

Hal Fī Dhālika Qasamun Lidhī Ĥijrin
Is there [not] in [all] that an oath [sufficient]
for one of perception? (5)

● ● ● ● ●

أَلَمْ تَرَ كَيْفَ فَعَلَ رَبُّكَ بِعَادٍ ﴿6﴾ 6

Alam Tara Kayfa Fa`ala Rabbuka Bi`ādin
Have you not considered how your Lord
dealt with 'Aad -(6)

إِرَمَ ذَاتِ الْعِمَادِ ﴿7﴾ 7

'Irama Dhāti Al-`Imādi

[With] Iram - who had lofty pillars, (7)

الَّتِي لَمْ يُخْلَقْ مِثْلُهَا فِي الْبِلَادِ ﴿8﴾ 8

Allatī Lam Yukhlaq Mithluhā Fī Al-Bilādi

The likes of whom had never been created in the land? (8)

وَثَمُودَ الَّذِينَ جَابُوا الصَّخْرَ بِالْوَادِ ﴿9﴾ 9

Wa Thamūda Al-Ladhīna Jābū Aş-Şakhra Bil-Wādi

And [with] Thamud, who carved out the rocks
in the valley? (9)

وَفِرْعَوْنَ ذِي الْأَوْتَادِ ﴿10﴾ 10

Wa Fir`awna Dhī Al-'Awtādi

And [with] Pharaoh, owner of the stakes? -(10)

الَّذِينَ طَغَوْا فِي الْبِلَادِ ﴿11﴾ 11

Al-Ladhīna Ţaghaw Fī Al-Bilādi

[All of] whom oppressed within the lands(11)

فَأَكْثَرُوا فِيهَا الْفَسَادَ ﴿12﴾ 12

Fa'aktharū Fīhā Al-Fasāda

And increased therein the corruption. (12)

فَصَبَّ عَلَيْهِمْ رَبُّكَ سَوْطَ عَذَابٍ ﴿13﴾ 13

Faşabba `Alayhim Rabbuka Sawţa `Adhābin
So your Lord poured upon them a scourge
of punishment. (13)

● ● ● ●

إِنَّ رَبَّكَ لَبِالْمِرْصَادِ ﴿14﴾ 14

Inna Rabbaka Labiālmirşādi
Indeed, your Lord is in observation.(14)

● ● ● ●

فَأَمَّا الْإِنسَانُ إِذَا مَا ابْتَلَاهُ رَبُّهُ فَأَكْرَمَهُ وَنَعَّمَهُ فَيَقُولُ رَبِّي أَكْرَمَنِ ﴿15﴾ 15

Fa'ammā Al-'Insānu 'Idhā Mā Abtalāhu Rabbuhu
Fa'akramahu Wa Na``amahu Fayaqūlu Rabbī 'Akramani
And as for man, when his Lord tries him and [thus]
is generous to him and favors him, he says,
"My Lord has honored me." (15)

● ● ● ●

وَأَمَّا إِذَا مَا ابْتَلَاهُ فَقَدَرَ عَلَيْهِ رِزْقَهُ فَيَقُولُ رَبِّي أَهَانَنِ ﴿16﴾ 16

Wa 'Ammā 'Idhā Mā Abtalāhu Faqadara `Alayhi
Rizqahu Fayaqūlu Rabbī 'Ahānani
But when He tries him and restricts his provision,
he says, "My Lord has humiliated me.""(16)

● ● ● ●

كَلَّا بَل لَّا تُكْرِمُونَ الْيَتِيمَ ﴿17﴾ 17

Kallā Bal Lā Tukrimūna Al-Yatīma
No! But you do not honor the orphan (17)

وَلَا تَحَاضُّونَ عَلَىٰ طَعَامِ الْمِسْكِينِ ﴿18﴾ 18

Wa Lā Taĥāđđūna `Alá Ţa`āmi Al-Miskīni
And you do not encourage one another to feed
the poor. (18)

• • •

وَتَأْكُلُونَ التُّرَاثَ أَكْلًا لَّمًّا ﴿19﴾ 19

Wa Ta'kulūna At-Turātha 'Aklāan Lammāan
And you consume inheritance, devouring
[it] altogether,(19)

• • • •

وَتُحِبُّونَ الْمَالَ حُبًّا جَمًّا ﴿20﴾ 20

Wa Tuĥibbūna Al-Māla Ĥubbāan Jammāan
And you love wealth with immense love.(20)

• • •

كَلَّا إِذَا دُكَّتِ الْأَرْضُ دَكًّا دَكًّا ﴿21﴾ 21

Kallā 'Idhā Dukkati Al-'Arđu Dakkāan Dakkāan
No! When the earth has been leveled - pounded
and crushed - (21)

• • • •

وَجَاءَ رَبُّكَ وَالْمَلَكُ صَفًّا صَفًّا ﴿22﴾ 22

Wa Jā'a Rabbuka Wa Al-Malaku Şaffāan Şaffāan
And your Lord has come and the angels, rank
upon rank,(22)

• • • •

وَجِيءَ يَوْمَئِذٍ بِجَهَنَّمَ يَوْمَئِذٍ يَتَذَكَّرُ الْإِنْسَانُ وَأَنَّىٰ لَهُ الذِّكْرَى ﴿23﴾ 23

Wa Jī'a Yawma'idhin Bijahannama Yawma'idhin
Yatadhakkaru Al-'Insānu Wa 'Anná Lahu Adh-Dhikrá
And brought [within view], that Day, is Hell - that Day, man
will remember, but what good to him will be th
remembrance?(23)

• • • • •

يَقُولُ يَا لَيْتَنِي قَدَّمْتُ لِحَيَاتِي ﴿24﴾24

Yaqūlu Yā Laytanī Qaddamtu Liḥayātī
He will say, "Oh, I wish I had sent ahead [some good]
for my life." (24)

• • • • •

فَيَوْمَئِذٍ لَّا يُعَذِّبُ عَذَابَهُ أَحَدٌ ﴿25﴾25

Fayawma'idhin Lā Yu`adhibu `Adhābahu 'Aḥadun
So on that Day, none will punish [as severely] as
His punishment,(25)

• • • • •

وَلَا يُوثِقُ وَثَاقَهُ أَحَدٌ ﴿26﴾26

Wa Lā Yūthiqu Wathāqahu 'Aḥadun
And none will bind [as severely] as His binding
[of the evildoers]. (26)

• • • • •

يَا أَيَّتُهَا النَّفْسُ الْمُطْمَئِنَّةُ ﴿27﴾27

Yā 'Ayyatuhā An-Nafsu Al-Muṭma'innahu
[To the righteous it will be said], "O reassured soul,(27)

• • • • •

ارْجِعِي إِلَى رَبِّكِ رَاضِيَةً مَّرْضِيَّةً ﴿28﴾28

Arji`ī 'Ilá Rabbiki Rāḍiyatan Marḍīyahan
[To the righteous it will be said], "O reassured soul,(28)

فَادْخُلِي فِي عِبَادِي ﴿29﴾ 29

Fādkhulī Fī `Ibādī
And enter among My [righteous] servants(29)

• • • •

وَادْخُلِي جَنَّتِي ﴿30﴾ 30

Wa Adkhulī Jannatī
And enter My Paradise."(30)

سُورَةُ البَلَد
Sourate Al-Balad

Bismi Allāhi Ar-Raḥmāni Ar-Raḥīmi   بِسْمِ اللهِ الرَّحْمَنِ الرَّحِيمِ

لَا أُقْسِمُ بِهَذَا الْبَلَدِ ﴿1﴾ 1

Lā 'Uqsimu Bihadhā Al-Baladi
I swear by this city, Makkah - (1)

• • • •

وَأَنتَ حِلٌّ بِهَذَا الْبَلَدِ ﴿2﴾ 2

Wa 'Anta Ḥillun Bihadhā Al-Baladi
And you, [O Muhammad], are free of restriction
in this city - (2)

• • • •

وَوَالِدٍ وَمَا وَلَدَ ﴿3﴾ 3

Wa Wālidin Wa Mā Walada
And [by] the father and that which was born [of him], (3)

• • • •

لَقَدْ خَلَقْنَا الْإِنسَانَ فِي كَبَدٍ ﴿4﴾ 4

Laqad Khalaqnā Al-'Insāna Fī Kabadin
We have certainly created man into hardship. (4)

أَيَحْسَبُ أَن لَّن يَقْدِرَ عَلَيْهِ أَحَدٌ ﴿5﴾ 5

Ayaĥsabu 'An Lan Yaqdira `Alayhi 'Aĥadun

Does he think that never will anyon overcome him? (5)

• • • •

يَقُولُ أَهْلَكْتُ مَالًا لُّبَدًا ﴿6﴾ 6

Yaqūlu 'Ahlaktu Mālāan Lubadāan

He says, "I have spent wealth in abundance." (6)

• • • •

أَيَحْسَبُ أَن لَّمْ يَرَهُ أَحَدٌ ﴿7﴾ 7

Ayaĥsabu 'An Lam Yarahu 'Aĥadun

Does he think that no one has seen him? (7)

• • • •

أَلَمْ نَجْعَل لَّهُ عَيْنَيْنِ ﴿8﴾ 8

Alam Naj`al Lahu `Aynayni

Have We not made for him two eyes? (8)

• • • •

وَلِسَانًا وَشَفَتَيْنِ ﴿9﴾ 9

Wa Lisānāan Wa Shafatayni

And a tongue and two lips? (9)

• • • •

وَهَدَيْنَاهُ النَّجْدَيْنِ ﴿10﴾ 10

Wa Hadaynāhu An-Najdayni

And have shown him the two ways? (10)

• • • •

فَلَا اقْتَحَمَ الْعَقَبَةَ ﴿11﴾ 11

Falā Aqtaĥama Al-`Aqabata

But he has not broken through the difficult pass.(11)

وَمَا أَدْرَاكَ مَا الْعَقَبَةُ ﴿12﴾ 12

Wa Mā 'Adrāka Mā Al-`Aqabatu

And what can make you know what is [breaking through]
the difficult pass? (12)

فَكُّ رَقَبَةٍ ﴿13﴾ 13

Fakku Raqabatin

It is the freeing of a slave(13)

أَوْ إِطْعَامٌ فِي يَوْمٍ ذِي مَسْغَبَةٍ ﴿14﴾ 14

'Aw 'Iṭ`āmun Fī Yawmin Dhī Masghabatin

Or feeding on a day of severe hunger (14)

يَتِيمًا ذَا مَقْرَبَةٍ ﴿15﴾ 15

Yatīmāan Dhā Maqrabatin

An orphan of near relationship (15)

أَوْ مِسْكِينًا ذَا مَتْرَبَةٍ ﴿16﴾ 16

'Aw Miskīnāan Dhā Matrabatin

Or a needy person in misery (16)

ثُمَّ كَانَ مِنَ الَّذِينَ آمَنُوا وَتَوَاصَوْا بِالصَّبْرِ وَتَوَاصَوْا بِالْمَرْحَمَةِ ﴿17﴾ 17

Thumma Kāna Mina Al-Ladhīna 'Āmanū Wa
Tawāṣaw Biṣ-Ṣabri Wa Tawāṣaw Bil-Marḥamati

And then being among those who believed
and advised one another to patience and advised
one another to compassion. (17)

أُوْلَئِكَ أَصْحَابُ الْمَيْمَنَةِ ﴿18﴾ 18

Ūlā'ika 'Aşḩābu Al-Maymanati

Those are the companions of the right. (18)

وَالَّذِينَ كَفَرُوا بِآيَاتِنَا هُمْ أَصْحَابُ الْمَشْأَمَةِ ﴿19﴾ 19

Wa Al-Ladhīna Kafarū Bi'āyātinā Hum 'Aşḩābu
Al-Mash'amati

But they who disbelieved in Our signs
those are the companions of the left. (19)

عَلَيْهِمْ نَارٌ مُّؤْصَدَةٌ ﴿20﴾ 20

`Alayhim Nārun Mu'uşadatun

Over them will be fire closed in.(20)

سُورَةُ الشَّمس
Sourate Ash-Shams

Bismi Allāhi Ar-Raḩmāni Ar-Raḩīmi   بِسْمِ اللهِ الرَّحْمَنِ الرَّحِيمِ

وَالشَّمْسِ وَضُحَاهَا ﴿1﴾ 1

Wa Ash-Shamsi Wa Đuḩāhā

By the sun and its brightness (1)

وَالْقَمَرِ إِذَا تَلَاهَا ﴿2﴾ 2

Wa Al-Qamari 'Idhā Talāhā

And [by] the moon when it follows it (2)

وَالنَّهَارِ إِذَا جَلَّاهَا ﴿3﴾ 3

Wa An-Nahāri 'Idhā Jallāhā

And [by] the day when it displays it (3)

وَاللَّيْلِ إِذَا يَغْشَاهَا ﴿4﴾ 4

Wa Al-Layli 'Idhā Yaghshāhā

And [by] the night when it covers it

وَالسَّمَاء وَمَا بَنَاهَا ﴿5﴾ 5

Wa As-Samā'i Wa Mā Banāhā

And [by] the sky and He who constructed it (5)

وَالْأَرْضِ وَمَا طَحَاهَا ﴿6﴾ 6

Wa Al-'Arđi Wa Mā Ţaĥāhā

And [by] the earth and He who spread it(6)

وَنَفْسٍ وَمَا سَوَّاهَا ﴿7﴾ 7

Wa Nafsin Wa Mā Sawwāhā

And [by] the soul and He who proportioned it(7)

فَأَلْهَمَهَا فُجُورَهَا وَتَقْوَاهَا ﴿8﴾ 8

Fa'alhamahā Fujūrahā Wa Taqwāhā

And inspired it [with discernment of] its wickedness
and its righteousness,(8)

قَد أَفْلَحَ مَن زَكَّاهَا ﴾9﴿9

Qad 'Aflaḥa Man Zakkāhā

He has succeeded who purifies it, (9)

●●●●●

وَقَد خَابَ مَن دَسَّاهَا ﴾10﴿10

Wa Qad Khāba Man Dassāhā

And he has failed who instills it [with corruption]. (10)

●●●●●

كَذَّبَت ثَمُودُ بِطَغْوَاهَا ﴾11﴿11

Kadhabat Thamūdu Biṭaghwāhā

Thamud denied [their prophet] by reason of their transgression, (11)

●●●●●

إِذِ انبَعَثَ أَشْقَاهَا ﴾12﴿12

'Idhi Anba`atha 'Ashqāhā

When the most wretched of them was sent forth. (12)

●●●●●

فَقَالَ لَهُمْ رَسُولُ اللَّهِ نَاقَةَ اللَّهِ وَسُقْيَاهَا ﴾13﴿13

Faqāla Lahum Rasūlu Allāhi Nāqata Allāhi Wa Suqyāhā

And the messenger of Allah [Salih] said to them, "[Do not harm] the she-camel of Allah or [prevent her from] her drink." (13)

●●●●●

فَكَذَّبُوهُ فَعَقَرُوهَا فَدَمْدَمَ عَلَيْهِمْ رَبُّهُم بِذَنبِهِمْ فَسَوَّاهَا ﴾14﴿14

Fakadhabūhu Fa`aqarūhā Fadamdama `Alayhim Rabbuhum Bidhanbihim Fasawwāhā

But they denied him and hamstrung her. So their Lord brought down upon them destruction for their sin and made it equal [upon all of them].. (14)

وَلَا يَخَافُ عُقْبَاهَا ﴿15﴾ 15

Wa Lā Yakhāfu `Uqbāhā

And He does not fear the consequence thereof. (15)

سورة الليل
Sourate Al-Layl

بِسْمِ اللَّهِ الرَّحْمَٰنِ الرَّحِيمِ Bismi Allāhi Ar-Raĥmāni Ar-Raĥīmi

وَاللَّيْلِ إِذَا يَغْشَى ﴿1﴾ 1

Wa Al-Layli 'Idhā Yaghshá

And He does not fear the consequence thereof. (1)

• • • • •

وَالنَّهَارِ إِذَا تَجَلَّى ﴿2﴾ 2

Wa An-Nahāri 'Idhā Tajallá

And [by] the day when it appears (2)

• • • • •

وَمَا خَلَقَ الذَّكَرَ وَالْأُنثَى ﴿3﴾ 3

Wa Mā Khalaqa Adh-Dhakara Wa Al-'Unthá

And [by] He who created the male and female, (3)

• • • • •

إِنَّ سَعْيَكُمْ لَشَتَّى ﴿4﴾ 4

'Inna Sa`yakum Lashattá

Indeed, your efforts are diverse. (4)

• • • • •

فَأَمَّا مَنْ أَعْطَى وَاتَّقَى ﴿5﴾ 5

Fa'ammā Man 'A`ţá Wa Attaqá

As for he who gives and fears Allah (5)

وَصَدَّقَ بِالْحُسْنَى ﴿6﴾ 6

Wa Şaddaqa Bil-Ĥusná

And believes in the best [reward], (6)

فَسَنُيَسِّرُهُ لِلْيُسْرَى ﴿7﴾ 7

Fasanuyassiruhu Lilyusrá

We will ease him toward ease. (7)

وَأَمَّا مَن بَخِلَ وَاسْتَغْنَى ﴿8﴾ 8

Wa 'Ammā Man Bakhila Wa Astaghná

But as for he who withholds and considers himself free of need(8)

وَكَذَّبَ بِالْحُسْنَى ﴿9﴾ 9

Wa Kadhaba Bil-Ĥusná

And denies the best [reward], (9)

فَسَنُيَسِّرُهُ لِلْعُسْرَى ﴿10﴾ 10

Fasanuyassiruhu Lil`usrá

We will ease him toward difficulty. (10)

وَمَا يُغْنِي عَنْهُ مَالُهُ إِذَا تَرَدَّى ﴿11﴾ 11

Wa Mā Yughnī `Anhu Māluhu 'Idhā Taraddá

And what will his wealth avail him when he falls?(11)

إِنَّ عَلَيْنَا لَلْهُدَى ﴿12﴾ 12

Inna `Alaynā Lalhudá

Indeed, [incumbent] upon Us is guidance.(12)

وَإِنَّ لَنَا لَلْآخِرَةَ وَالْأُولَى ﴿13﴾ 13

Wa 'Inna Lanā Lal'ākhirata Wa Al-'Ūlá

And indeed, to Us belongs the Hereafter and the first [life].(13)

فَأَنذَرْتُكُمْ نَارًا تَلَظَّى ﴿14﴾ 14

Fa'andhartukum Nārāan Talažžá

So I have warned you of a Fire which is blazing.(14)

لَا يَصْلَاهَا إِلَّا الْأَشْقَى ﴿15﴾ 15

Lā Yaşlāhā 'Illā Al-'Ashqá

None will [enter to] burn therein except the most wretched one.(15)

الَّذِي كَذَّبَ وَتَوَلَّى ﴿16﴾ 16

Al-Ladhī Kadhaba Wa Tawallá

Who had denied and turned away.(16)

وَسَيُجَنَّبُهَا الْأَتْقَى ﴿17﴾ 17

Wa Sayujannabuhā Al-'Atqá

But the righteous one will avoid it - (17)

الَّذِي يُؤْتِي مَالَهُ يَتَزَكَّى ﴿18﴾ 18

Al-Ladhī Yu'utī Mālahu Yatazakká

[He] who gives [from] his wealth to purify himself (18)

وَمَا لِأَحَدٍ عِندَهُ مِن نِّعْمَةٍ تُجْزَى ﴿19﴾ 19

Wa Mā Li'ĥadin `Indahu Min Ni`matin Tujzá

And not [giving] for anyone who has [done him]
a favor to be rewarded (19)

● ● ● ● ●

إِلَّا ابْتِغَاءَ وَجْهِ رَبِّهِ الْأَعْلَى ﴿20﴾ 20

'Illā Abtighā'a Wajhi Rabbihi Al-'A`lá

But only seeking the countenance of his Lord,
Most High. (20)

● ● ● ● ●

وَلَسَوْفَ يَرْضَى ﴿21﴾ 21

Wa Lasawfa Yarđá

And he is going to be satisfied. (21)

سورة الضحى
Sourate Ad-Duha

Bismi Allāhi Ar-Raĥmāni Ar-Raĥīmi
بِسْمِ اللهِ الرَّحْمَنِ الرَّحِيمِ

وَالضُّحَى ﴿1﴾ 1

Wa Ađ-Đuĥá

By the morning brightness (1)

● ● ● ● ●

وَاللَّيْلِ إِذَا سَجَى ﴿2﴾ 2

Wa Al-Layli 'Idhā Sajá

And [by] the night when it covers with darkness, (2)

● ● ● ● ●

مَا وَدَّعَكَ رَبُّكَ وَمَا قَلَى ﴿3﴾ 3

Mā Wadda`aka Rabbuka Wa Mā Qalá

Your Lord has not taken leave of you, [O Muhammad], nor
has He detested [you]. (3)

● ● ● ● ●

28

وَلَلْآخِرَةُ خَيْرٌ لَّكَ مِنَ الْأُولَى ﴿4﴾

Wa Lal'ākhiratu Khayrun Laka Mina Al-'Ūlá

And the Hereafter is better for you than
the first [life].(4)

• • • • •

وَلَسَوْفَ يُعْطِيكَ رَبُّكَ فَتَرْضَى ﴿5﴾

Wa Lasawfa Yu`ṭīka Rabbuka Fataráá

And your Lord is going to give you, and you
will be satisfied.(5)

• • • • •

أَلَمْ يَجِدْكَ يَتِيمًا فَآوَى ﴿6﴾

Alam Yajidka Yatīmāan Fa'āwá

Did He not find you an orphan and give [you] refuge? (6)

• • • • •

وَوَجَدَكَ ضَالًّا فَهَدَى ﴿7﴾

Wa Wajadaka Ðāllāan Fahadá

And He found you lost and guided [you],(7)

• • • • •

وَوَجَدَكَ عَائِلًا فَأَغْنَى ﴿8﴾

Wa Wajadaka `Ā'ilāan Fa'aghná

And He found you poor and made [you] self-sufficient. (8)

• • • • •

فَأَمَّا الْيَتِيمَ فَلَا تَقْهَرْ ﴿9﴾

Fa'ammā Al-Yatīma Falā Taqhar

So as for the orphan, do not oppress [him]. (9)

• • • • •

وَأَمَّا السَّائِلَ فَلَا تَنْهَرْ ﴿10﴾ 10

Wa 'Ammā As-Sā'ila Falā Tanhar

And as for the petitioner, do not repel [him].(10)

• • • •

وَأَمَّا بِنِعْمَةِ رَبِّكَ فَحَدِّثْ ﴿11﴾ 11

Wa 'Ammā Bini`mati Rabbika Faĥaddith

But as for the favor of your Lord, report [it]. (11)

سورة الشرح
Surah Ash-Sharh

Bismi Allāhi Ar-Raĥmāni Ar-Raĥīmi

بِسْمِ اللهِ الرَّحْمَنِ الرَّحِيمِ

أَلَمْ نَشْرَحْ لَكَ صَدْرَكَ ﴿1﴾ 1

'Alam Nashraĥ Laka Şadraka

Did We not expand for you, [O Muhammad], your breast? (1)

• • • •

وَوَضَعْنَا عَنكَ وِزْرَكَ ﴿2﴾ 2

Wa Waḍa`nā `Anka Wizraka

And We removed from you your burden (2)

• • • •

الَّذِي أَنقَضَ ظَهْرَكَ ﴿3﴾ 3

Al-Ladhī 'Anqaḍa Žahraka

Which had weighed upon your back (3)

• • • •

30

وَرَفَعْنَا لَكَ ذِكْرَكَ ﴿4﴾ 4

Wa Rafa`nā Laka Dhikraka

And raised high for you your repute.(4)

● ● ● ● ●

فَإِنَّ مَعَ الْعُسْرِ يُسْرًا ﴿5﴾ 5

Fa'inna Ma`a Al-`Usri Yusrāan

For indeed, with hardship [will be] ease. (5)

● ● ● ● ●

إِنَّ مَعَ الْعُسْرِ يُسْرًا ﴿6﴾ 6

Inna Ma`a Al-`Usri Yusrāan

Indeed, with hardship [will be] ease. (6)

● ● ● ● ●

فَإِذَا فَرَغْتَ فَانصَبْ ﴿7﴾ 7

Fa'idhā Faraghta Fānşab

So when you have finished [your duties], then stand up
[for worship]. (7)

● ● ● ● ●

وَإِلَى رَبِّكَ فَارْغَبْ ﴿8﴾ 8

Wa 'Ilá Rabbika Fārghab

And to your Lord direct [your] longing. (8)

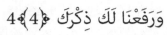

سورة التين
Sourate At-Tin

Bismi Allāhi Ar-Raĥmāni Ar-Raĥīmi   بِسْمِ اللهِ الرَّحْمَنِ الرَّحِيمِ

وَالتِّينِ وَالزَّيْتُونِ ﴿1﴾ 1

Wa At-Tīni Wa Az-Zaytūni

By the fig and the olive (1)

وَطُورِ سِينِينَ ﴿2﴾ 2

Wa Ṭūri Sīnīna

And [by] Mount Sinai (2)

وَهَذَا الْبَلَدِ الْأَمِينِ ﴿3﴾ 3

Wa Hadhā Al-Baladi Al-'Amīni

And [by] this secure city [Makkah], (3)

لَقَدْ خَلَقْنَا الْإِنسَانَ فِي أَحْسَنِ تَقْوِيمٍ ﴿4﴾ 4

Laqad Khalaqnā Al-'Insāna Fī 'Aḥsani Taqwīmin

We have certainly created man in the best of stature;

ثُمَّ رَدَدْنَاهُ أَسْفَلَ سَافِلِينَ ﴿5﴾ 5

Thumma Radadnāhu 'Asfala Sāfilīna

Then We return him to the lowest of the low, (5)

إِلَّا الَّذِينَ آمَنُوا وَعَمِلُوا الصَّالِحَاتِ فَلَهُمْ أَجْرٌ غَيْرُ مَمْنُونٍ ﴿6﴾ 3

'Illā Al-Ladhīna 'Āmanū Wa `Amilū Aṣ-Ṣāliḥāti
Falahum 'Ajrun Ghayru Mamnūnin

Except for those who believe and do righteous deeds, for they will have a reward uninterrupted.

● ● ● ●

فَمَا يُكَذِّبُكَ بَعْدُ بِالدِّينِ ﴿7﴾ 7

Famā Yukadhibuka Ba`du Bid-Dīni

So what yet causes you to deny the Recompense? (7)

● ● ● ●

أَلَيْسَ اللَّهُ بِأَحْكَمِ الْحَاكِمِينَ ﴿8﴾ 8

Alaysa Allāhu Bi'aĥkami Al-Ĥākimīna

Is not Allah the most just of judges? (8)

سورة العلق
Sourate Al-'Alaq

Bismi Allāhi Ar-Raĥmāni Ar-Raĥīmi   بِسْمِ اللَّهِ الرَّحْمَٰنِ الرَّحِيمِ

اقْرَأْ بِاسْمِ رَبِّكَ الَّذِي خَلَقَ ﴿1﴾ 1

Iqra' Biāsmi Rabbika Al-Ladhī Khalaqa

Recite in the name of your Lord who created - (1)

● ● ● ●

خَلَقَ الْإِنْسَانَ مِنْ عَلَقٍ ﴿2﴾ 2

Khalaqa Al-'Insāna Min `Alaqin

Created man from a clinging substance. (2)

● ● ● ●

اقْرَأْ وَرَبُّكَ الْأَكْرَمُ ﴿3﴾ 3

Iqra' Wa Rabbuka Al-'Akramu

Recite, and your Lord is the most Generous - (3)

الَّذِي عَلَّمَ بِالْقَلَمِ ﴿4﴾ 4

Al-Ladhī `Allama Bil-Qalami

Who taught by the pen - (4)

عَلَّمَ الْإِنسَانَ مَا لَمْ يَعْلَمْ ﴿5﴾ 5

`Allama Al-'Insāna Mā Lam Ya`lam

Taught man that which he knew not. (5)

كَلَّا إِنَّ الْإِنسَانَ لَيَطْغَى ﴿6﴾ 6

Kallā 'Inna Al-'Insāna Layaţghá

No! [But] indeed, man transgresses (6)

أَن رَّآهُ اسْتَغْنَى ﴿7﴾ 7

'An Ra'āhu Astaghná

Because he sees himself self-sufficient. (7)

إِنَّ إِلَى رَبِّكَ الرُّجْعَى ﴿8﴾ 8

Inna 'Ilá Rabbika Ar-Ruj`á

Indeed, to your Lord is the return. (8)

أَرَأَيْتَ الَّذِي يَنْهَى ﴿9﴾ 9

'Ara'ayta Al-Ladhī Yanhá

Have you seen the one who forbids (9)

عَبْدًا إِذَا صَلَّى ﴿10﴾ 10

`Abdāan 'Idhā Şallá

A servant when he prays? (10)

أَرَأَيْتَ إِن كَانَ عَلَى الْهُدَى ﴿11﴾ 11

Ara'ayta 'In Kāna `Alá Al-Hudá

Have you seen if he is upon guidance

● ● ●

أَوْ أَمَرَ بِالتَّقْوَى ﴿12﴾ 12

Aw 'Amara Bit-Taqwá

Or enjoins righteousness? (12)

● ● ●

أَرَأَيْتَ إِن كَذَّبَ وَتَوَلَّى ﴿13﴾ 13

'Ara'ayta 'In Kadhaba Wa Tawallá

Have you seen if he denies and turns away - (13)

● ● ●

أَلَمْ يَعْلَمْ بِأَنَّ اللَّهَ يَرَى ﴿14﴾ 14

Alam Ya`lam Bi'anna Allāha Yará

Does he not know that Allah sees? (14)

● ● ●

كَلَّا لَئِن لَّمْ يَنتَهِ لَنَسْفَعًا بِالنَّاصِيَةِ ﴿15﴾ 15

Kallā La'in Lam Yantahi Lanasfa`ā Bin-Nāşiyati

No! If he does not desist, We will surely drag him by the forelock - (15)

● ● ●

نَاصِيَةٍ كَاذِبَةٍ خَاطِئَةٍ ﴿16﴾ 16

Nāşiyatin Kādhibatin Khāţi'atin

A lying, sinning forelock. (16)

● ● ●

فَلْيَدْعُ نَادِيَه ﴿17﴾ 17

Falyad`u Nādiyah

Then let him call his associates; (17)

● ● ●

سَنَدْعُ الزَّبَانِيَةَ ﴿18﴾ 18

Sanad`u Az-Zabāniyata

We will call the angels of Hell.18)

● ● ●

35

كَلَّا لَا تُطِعْهُ وَاسْجُدْ وَاقْتَرِبْ ۩ ﴿19﴾ 19

Kallā Lā Tuṭi`hu Wa Asjud Wāqtarib

No! Do not obey him. But prostrate and draw
near [to Allah]. (19)

سورة القدر
Sourate Al-Qadr

Bismi Allāhi Ar-Raḥmāni Ar-Raḥīmi   بِسْمِ اللَّهِ الرَّحْمَنِ الرَّحِيمِ

إِنَّا أَنزَلْنَاهُ فِي لَيْلَةِ الْقَدْرِ ﴿1﴾ 1

Innā 'Anzalnāhu Fī Laylati Al-Qadri

Indeed, We sent the Qur'an down during
the Night of Decree. (1)

● ● ● ●

وَمَا أَدْرَاكَ مَا لَيْلَةُ الْقَدْرِ ﴿2﴾ 2

Wa Mā 'Adrāka Mā Laylatu Al-Qadri

And what can make you know what is the Night
of Decree? (2)

● ● ● ●

لَيْلَةُ الْقَدْرِ خَيْرٌ مِّنْ أَلْفِ شَهْرٍ ﴿3﴾ 3

Laylatu Al-Qadri Khayrun Min 'Alfi Shahrin

The Night of Decree is better than a thousand
months. (3)

● ● ● ●

تَنَزَّلُ الْمَلَائِكَةُ وَالرُّوحُ فِيهَا بِإِذْنِ رَبِّهِم مِّن كُلِّ أَمْرٍ ﴿4﴾ 4

Tanazzalu Al-Malā'ikatu Wa Ar-Rūḥu Fīhā Bi'idhni Rabbihim Min Kulli 'Amrin

The angels and the Spirit descend therein by permission of their Lord for every matter. (4)

● ● ● ● ●

سَلَامٌ هِيَ حَتَّى مَطْلَعِ الْفَجْرِ ﴿5﴾5

Salāmun Hiya Ĥattá Maṭla`i Al-Fajri

Peace it is until the emergence of dawn. (5)

سورة البينة
Sourate Al-Bayyinah

Bismi Allāhi Ar-Raĥmāni Ar-Raĥīmi بِسْمِ اللهِ الرَّحْمَنِ الرَّحِيمِ

لَمْ يَكُنِ الَّذِينَ كَفَرُوا مِنْ أَهْلِ الْكِتَابِ وَالْمُشْرِكِينَ مُنفَكِّينَ حَتَّى تَأْتِيَهُمُ الْبَيِّنَةُ ﴿1﴾1 َ

Lam Yakuni Al-Ladhīna Kafarū Min 'Ahli Al-Kitābi Wa Al-Mushrikīna Munfakkīna Ĥattá Ta'tiyahumu Al-Bayyinatu

Those who disbelieved among the People of the Scripture and the polytheists were not to be parted [from misbelief] until there came to them clear evidence -

● ● ● ● ●

رَسُولٌ مِّنَ اللهِ يَتْلُو صُحُفًا مُّطَهَّرَةً ﴿2﴾2

Rasūlun Mina Allāhi Yatlū Şuĥufāan Muţahharatan

A Messenger from Allah , reciting purified scriptures (2)

● ● ● ●

فِيهَا كُتُبٌ قَيِّمَةٌ ﴿3﴾3

Fīhā Kutubun Qayyimatun
Within which are correct writings. (3)

وَمَا تَفَرَّقَ الَّذِينَ أُوتُوا الْكِتَابَ إِلَّا مِن بَعْدِ مَا جَاءَتْهُمُ الْبَيِّنَةُ ﴿4﴾

Wa Mā Tafarraqa Al-Ladhīna 'Ūtū Al-Kitāba 'Illā Min
Ba`di Mā Jā'athumu Al-Bayyinatu
Nor did those who were given the Scripture
become divided until after there had come to them
clear evidence.(4)

وَمَا أُمِرُوا إِلَّا لِيَعْبُدُوا اللَّهَ مُخْلِصِينَ لَهُ الدِّينَ حُنَفَاء وَيُقِيمُوا
الصَّلَاةَ وَيُؤْتُوا الزَّكَاةَ وَذَلِكَ دِينُ الْقَيِّمَةِ ﴿5﴾

Wa Mā 'Umirū 'Illā Liya`budū Allāha Mukhlişīna Lahu
Ad-Dīna Ĥunafā'a Wa Yuqīmū Aş-Şalāata Wa Yu'utū Az-Zakāata
Wa Dhalika Dīnu Al-Qayyimati
And they were not commanded except to worship Allah ,
[being] sincere to Him in religion, inclining to truth,
and to establish prayer and to give zakah. And that
is the correct religion. (5)

إِنَّ الَّذِينَ كَفَرُوا مِنْ أَهْلِ الْكِتَابِ وَالْمُشْرِكِينَ فِي نَارِ جَهَنَّم
خَالِدِينَ فِيهَا أُوْلَئِكَ هُمْ شَرُّ الْبَرِيَّةِ ﴿6﴾

'Inna Al-Ladhīna Kafarū Min 'Ahli Al-Kitābi Wa Al-Mushrikīna
Fī Nāri Jahannama Khālidīna Fīhā 'Ūlā'ika Hum Sharru Al-Barīyati
Indeed, they who disbelieved among the People of
the Scripture and the polytheists will be in the fire of Hell,
abiding eternally therein. Those are the worst of creatures. (6)

إِنَّ الَّذِينَ آمَنُوا وَعَمِلُوا الصَّالِحَاتِ أُولَئِكَ هُمْ خَيْرُ الْبَرِيَّةِ ﴿7﴾

'Inna Al-Ladhīna 'Āmanū Wa `Amilū Aş-Şāliĥāti
'Ūlā'ika Hum Khayru Al-Barīyati
Indeed, they who have believed and done
righteous deeds - those are the best of creatures. (7)

جَزَاؤُهُمْ عِندَ رَبِّهِمْ جَنَّاتُ عَدْنٍ تَجْرِي مِن تَحْتِهَا الْأَنْهَارُ خَالِدِينَ فِيهَا
أَبَدًا رَّضِيَ اللَّهُ عَنْهُمْ وَرَضُوا عَنْهُ ذَلِكَ لِمَنْ خَشِيَ رَبَّهُ ﴿8﴾

Jazā'uuhum `Inda Rabbihim Jannātu `Adnin Tajrī Min
Taĥtihā Al-'Anhāru Khālidīna Fīhā 'Abadāan Rađiya Allāhu
`Anhum Wa Rađū `Anhu Dhālika Liman Khashiya Rabbahu
Their reward with Allah will be gardens of perpetual resi-
dence beneath which rivers flow, wherein they will abide
forever, Allah being pleased with them and they with Him.
That is for whoever has feared his Lord. (8)

سورة الزلزلة
Sourate Az-Zalzalah

Bismi Allāhi Ar-Raĥmāni Ar-Raĥīmi   بِسْمِ اللَّهِ الرَّحْمَنِ الرَّحِيمِ

إِذَا زُلْزِلَتِ الْأَرْضُ زِلْزَالَهَا ﴿1﴾

'Idhā Zulzilati Al-'Arđu Zilzālahā
When the earth is shaken with its [final] earthquake (1)

وَأَخْرَجَتِ الْأَرْضُ أَثْقَالَهَا ﴿2﴾ 2

Wa 'Akhrajati Al-'Arḍu 'Athqālahā
And the earth discharges its burdens. (2)

وَقَالَ الْإِنسَانُ مَا لَهَا ﴿3﴾ 3

Wa Qāla Al-'Insānu Mā Lahā
And man says, "What is [wrong] with it?" - (3)

يَوْمَئِذٍ تُحَدِّثُ أَخْبَارَهَا ﴿4﴾ 4

Yawma'idhin Tuḥaddithu 'Akhbārahā
That Day, it will report its news

بِأَنَّ رَبَّكَ أَوْحَى لَهَا ﴿5﴾ 5

Bi'anna Rabbaka 'Awḥá Lahā
Because your Lord has commanded it. (5)

يَوْمَئِذٍ يَصْدُرُ النَّاسُ أَشْتَاتًا لِّيُرَوْا أَعْمَالَهُمْ ﴿6﴾ 6

Yawma'idhin Yaṣduru An-Nāsu 'Ashtātāan
Liyuraw 'A`mālahum
That Day, the people will depart separated [into categories]
to be shown [the result of] their deeds. (6)

فَمَن يَعْمَلْ مِثْقَالَ ذَرَّةٍ خَيْرًا يَرَهُ ﴿7﴾ 7

Faman Ya`mal Mithqāla Dharratin Khayrāan Yarahu
So whoever does an atom's weight of good
will see it, (7)

وَمَن يَعْمَلْ مِثْقَالَ ذَرَّةٍ شَرًّا يَرَهُ ﴿8﴾ 8

Wa Man Ya`mal Mithqāla Dharratin Sharrāan Yarahu
So whoever does an atom's weight of good will see it, (8)

سورة العاديات
Sourate Al-Adiyat

Bismi Allāhi Ar-Raḥmāni Ar-Raḥīmi   

وَالْعَادِيَاتِ ضَبْحًا ﴿1﴾ 1

Wa Al-`Ādiyāti Đabḥāan
By the racers, panting, (1)

• • • •

فَالْمُورِيَاتِ قَدْحًا ﴿2﴾ 2

Fālmūriyāti Qadḥāan
And the producers of sparks [when] striking (2)

• • • •

فَالْمُغِيرَاتِ صُبْحًا ﴿3﴾ 3

Fālmughīrāti Ṣubḥāan
And the chargers at dawn, (3)

• • • •

فَأَثَرْنَ بِهِ نَقْعًا ﴿4﴾ 4

Fa'atharna Bihi Naq`āan
Stirring up thereby [clouds of] dust, (4)

• • • •

فَوَسَطْنَ بِهِ جَمْعًا ﴿5﴾ 5

Fawasaṭna Bihi Jam`āan
Arriving thereby in the center collectively, (5)

إِنَّ الْإِنسَانَ لِرَبِّهِ لَكَنُودٌ ﴿6﴾ 6

Inna Al-'Insāna Lirabbihi Lakanūdun
Indeed mankind, to his Lord, is ungrateful. (6)

وَإِنَّهُ عَلَى ذَلِكَ لَشَهِيدٌ ﴿7﴾ 7

Wa 'Innahu `Alá Dhālika Lashahīdun
And indeed, he is to that a witness. (7)

وَإِنَّهُ لِحُبِّ الْخَيْرِ لَشَدِيدٌ ﴿8﴾ 8

Wa 'Innahu Liḥubbi Al-Khayri Lashadīdun
And indeed he is, in love of wealth, intense. (8)

أَفَلَا يَعْلَمُ إِذَا بُعْثِرَ مَا فِي الْقُبُورِ ﴿9﴾ 9

'Afalā Ya`lamu 'Idhā Bu`thira Mā Fī Al-Qubūri
But does he not know that when the contents
of the graves are scattered(9)

وَحُصِّلَ مَا فِي الصُّدُورِ ﴿10﴾ 10

Wa Ĥuşşila Mā Fī Aş-Şudūri

And that within the breasts is obtained, (10)

إِنَّ رَبَّهُم بِهِمْ يَوْمَئِذٍ لَّخَبِيرٌ ﴿11﴾ 11

'Inna Rabbahum Bihim Yawma'idhin Lakhabīrun

Indeed, their Lord with them, that Day,
is [fully] Acquainted. (11)

سورة القارعة
Sourate Al-Qari'a

بِسْمِ اللَّهِ الرَّحْمَٰنِ الرَّحِيمِ

Bismi Allāhi Ar-Raĥmāni Ar-Raĥīmi

الْقَارِعَةُ ﴿1﴾ 1

Al-Qāri`atu
The Striking Calamity - (1)

مَا الْقَارِعَةُ ﴿2﴾ 2

Mā Al-Qāri`atu
What is the Striking Calamity? (2)

وَمَا أَدْرَاكَ مَا الْقَارِعَةُ ﴿3﴾ 3

Wa Mā 'Adrāka Mā Al-Qāri`atu
And what can make you know what is the Striking
Calamity?? (3)

يَوْمَ يَكُونُ النَّاسُ كَالْفَرَاشِ الْمَبْثُوثِ ﴿4﴾ 4

Yawma Yakūnu An-Nāsu Kālfarāshi Al-Mabthūthi

It is the Day when people will be like moths,
dispersed, (4)

وَتَكُونُ الْجِبَالُ كَالْعِهْنِ الْمَنفُوشِ ﴿5﴾ 5

Wa Takūnu Al-Jibālu Kāl`ihni Al-Manfūshi

And the mountains will be like wool, fluffed up. (5)

فَأَمَّا مَن ثَقُلَتْ مَوَازِينُهُ ﴿6﴾ 6

Fa'ammā Man Thaqulat Mawāzīnuhu

Then as for one whose scales are heavy
[with good deeds], (6)

فَهُوَ فِي عِيشَةٍ رَّاضِيَةٍ ﴿7﴾ 7

Fahuwa Fī `Īshatin Rāđiyatin

He will be in a pleasant life. (7)

وَأَمَّا مَنْ خَفَّتْ مَوَازِينُهُ ﴿8﴾ 8

Wa 'Ammā Man Khaffat Mawāzīnuhu

But as for one whose scales are light, (8)

فَأُمُّهُ هَاوِيَةٌ ﴿9﴾ 9

Fa'ummuhu Hāwiyatun
His refuge will be an abyss. (9)

وَمَا أَدْرَاكَ مَا هِيَهْ ﴿10﴾10

Wa Mā 'Adrāka Mā Hiyah
And what can make you know what that is? (10)

نَارٌ حَامِيَةٌ ﴿11﴾11

Nārun Ĥāmiyatun
It is a Fire, intensely hot. (11)

سورة التكاثر
Sourate At-Takathur

Bismi Allāhi Ar-Raĥmāni Ar-Raĥīmi   بِسْمِ اللهِ الرَّحْمَنِ الرَّحِيمِ

أَلْهَاكُمُ التَّكَاثُرُ ﴿1﴾1

'Alhākumu At-Takāthuru
Competition in [worldly] increase diverts you (1)

حَتَّى زُرْتُمُ الْمَقَابِرَ ﴿2﴾2

Ĥattá Zurtumu Al-Maqābira
Until you visit the graveyards. (2)

45

كَلَّا سَوْفَ تَعْلَمُونَ ﴿3﴾ 3

Kallā Sawfa Ta`lamūna

No! You are going to know. (3)

ثُمَّ كَلَّا سَوْفَ تَعْلَمُونَ ﴿4﴾ 4

Thumma Kallā Sawfa Ta`lamūna

Then no! You are going to know.(4)

كَلَّا لَوْ تَعْلَمُونَ عِلْمَ الْيَقِينِ ﴿5﴾ 5

Kallā Law Ta`lamūna `Ilma Al-Yaqīni

No! If you only knew with knowledge
of certainty... (5)

لَتَرَوُنَّ الْجَحِيمَ ﴿6﴾ 6

Latarawunna Al-Jaḥīma

You will surely see the Hellfire. (6)

ثُمَّ لَتَرَوُنَّهَا عَيْنَ الْيَقِينِ ﴿7﴾ 7

Thumma Latarawunnahā `Ayna Al-Yaqīni

Then you will surely see it with the eye
of certainty. (7)

ثُمَّ لَتُسْأَلُنَّ يَوْمَئِذٍ عَنِ النَّعِيمِ ﴿8﴾ 8

Thumma Latus'alunna Yawma'idhin `Ani An-Na`īmi

Then you will surely be asked that Day about
pleasure.(8)

سورة العصر
Sourate Al-Asr

Bismi Allāhi Ar-Raĥmāni Ar-Raĥīmi

بِسْمِ اللَّهِ الرَّحْمَٰنِ الرَّحِيمِ

وَالْعَصْرِ ﴿1﴾ 1

Wa Al-`Aşri

By time, (1)

• • • •

إِنَّ الْإِنسَانَ لَفِي خُسْرٍ ﴿2﴾ 2

'Inna Al-'Insāna Lafī Khusrin

Indeed, mankind is in loss, (2)

• • • •

إِلَّا الَّذِينَ آمَنُوا وَعَمِلُوا الصَّالِحَاتِ وَتَوَاصَوْا بِالْحَقِّ
وَتَوَاصَوْا بِالصَّبْرِ ﴿3﴾ 3

'Illā Al-Ladhīna 'Āmanū Wa `Amilū Aş-Şāliĥāti
Wa Tawāşaw Bil-Ĥaqqi Wa Tawāşaw Biş-Şabri

Except for those who have believed and done
righteous deeds and advised each other
to truth and advised each other to patience. (3)

سورة الهمزة
Sourate Al-Humazah

Bismi Allāhi Ar-Raĥmāni Ar-Raĥīmi

بِسْمِ اللَّهِ الرَّحْمَٰنِ الرَّحِيمِ

وَيْلٌ لِّكُلِّ هُمَزَةٍ لُّمَزَةٍ ﴿1﴾ 1

Waylun Likulli Humazatin Lumazatin

Woe to every scorner and mocker! (1)

الَّذِي جَمَعَ مَالًا وَعَدَّدَهُ ﴿2﴾ 2

Al-Ladhī Jama`a Mālāan Wa `Addadahu

Who collects wealth and [continuously] counts it. (2)

يَحْسَبُ أَنَّ مَالَهُ أَخْلَدَهُ ﴿3﴾ 3

Yaĥsabu 'Anna Mālahu 'Akhladahu

He thinks that his wealth will make him immortal.(3)

كَلَّا لَيُنبَذَنَّ فِي الْحُطَمَةِ ﴿4﴾ 4

Kallā Layunbadhanna Fī Al-Ĥuţamati

No! He will surely be thrown into the Crusher.(4)

وَمَا أَدْرَاكَ مَا الْحُطَمَةُ ﴿5﴾ 5

Wa Mā 'Adrāka Mā Al-Ĥuţamatu

And what can make you know what is the Crusher? (5)

نَارُ اللَّهِ الْمُوقَدَةُ ﴿6﴾ 6

Nāru Allāhi Al-Mūqadatu

It is the fire of Allah , [eternally] fueled, (6)

الَّتِي تَطَّلِعُ عَلَى الْأَفْئِدَةِ ﴿7﴾ 7

Allatī Taţţali`u `Alá Al-'Af'idati

Which mounts directed at the hearts.(7)

• • •

إِنَّهَا عَلَيْهِم مُّؤْصَدَةٌ ﴿8﴾ 8

Innahā `Alayhim Mu'uşadatun

Indeed, Hellfire will be closed down upon them (8)

• • • •

فِي عَمَدٍ مُّمَدَّدَةٍ ﴿9﴾ 9

Fī `Amadin Mumaddadatin

In extended columns.(9)

سورة الفيل
Sourate Al-Fîl

Bismi Allāhi Ar-Raḥmāni Ar-Raḥīmi   بِسْمِ اللهِ الرَّحْمٰنِ الرَّحِيمِ

أَلَمْ تَرَ كَيْفَ فَعَلَ رَبُّكَ بِأَصْحَابِ الْفِيلِ ﴿1﴾ 1

Alam Tará Kayfa Fa`ala Rabbuka Bi'aşḥābi Al-Fīl

Have you not considered, [O Muhammad], how your Lord dealt with the companions of the elephant?(1)

• • • •

أَلَمْ يَجْعَلْ كَيْدَهُمْ فِي تَضْلِيلٍ ﴿2﴾ 2

Alam Yaj`al Kaydahum Fī Taḍlīlin

Did He not make their plan into misguidance? (2)

• • • •

وَأَرْسَلَ عَلَيْهِمْ طَيْرًا أَبَابِيلَ ﴿3﴾ 3

Wa 'Arsala `Alayhim Ṭayrāan 'Abābīla
And He sent against them birds in flocks, (3)

تَرْمِيهِم بِحِجَارَةٍ مِّن سِجِّيلٍ ﴿4﴾4

Tarmīhim Biḥijāratin Min Sijjīlin
Striking them with stones of hard clay, (4)

فَجَعَلَهُمْ كَعَصْفٍ مَّأْكُولٍ ﴿5﴾5

Faja`alahum Ka`aṣfin Ma'kūlin
And He made them like eaten straw. (5)

سورة قريش
Sourate Quraysh

Bismi Allāhi Ar-Raḥmāni Ar-Raḥīmi
بِسْمِ اللَّهِ الرَّحْمَٰنِ الرَّحِيمِ

لِإِيلَافِ قُرَيْشٍ ﴿1﴾1

Li'īlāfi Qurayshin
For the accustomed security of the Quraysh - (1)

إِيلَافِهِمْ رِحْلَةَ الشِّتَاءِ وَالصَّيْفِ ﴿2﴾2

'Īlāfihim Riḥlata Ash-Shitā'i Wa Aṣ-Ṣayfi
Their accustomed security [in] the caravan
of winter and summer - (2)

فَلْيَعْبُدُوا رَبَّ هَذَا الْبَيْتِ ﴿3﴾3

Falya`budū Rabba Hādhā Al-Bayti

Let them worship the Lord of this House, (3)

الَّذِي أَطْعَمَهُم مِّن جُوعٍ وَآمَنَهُم مِّنْ خَوْفٍ ﴿4﴾4

Al-Ladhī 'Aţ`amahum Min Jū`in Wa 'Āmanahum Min Khawfin

Who has fed them, [saving them] from hunger and made them safe, [saving them] from fear.(4)

سورة الماعون
Sourate Al-Ma'un

Bismi Allāhi Ar-Raḥmāni Ar-Raḥīmi بِسْمِ اللهِ الرَّحْمَنِ الرَّحِيمِ

أَرَأَيْتَ الَّذِي يُكَذِّبُ بِالدِّينِ ﴿1﴾1

'Ara'ayta Al-Ladhī Yukadhibu Bid-Dīni

Have you seen the one who denies the Recompense?? (1)

فَذَلِكَ الَّذِي يَدُعُّ الْيَتِيمَ ﴿2﴾2

Fadhālika Al-Ladhī Yadu``u Al-Yatīma

For that is the one who drives away the orphan (2)

وَلَا يَحُضُّ عَلَى طَعَامِ الْمِسْكِينِ ﴿3﴾3

Wa Lā Yaḥuđđu `Alá Ţa`āmi Al-Miskīni

And does not encourage the feeding of the poor.

فَوَيْلٌ لِّلْمُصَلِّينَ ﴿4﴾ 4

Fawaylun Lilmuşallīna
So woe to those who pray(4)

●●●●●

الَّذِينَ هُمْ عَن صَلَاتِهِمْ سَاهُونَ ﴿5﴾ 5

Al-Ladhīna Hum `An Şalātihim Sāhūna
[But] who are heedless of their prayer - (5)

●●●●●

الَّذِينَ هُمْ يُرَاؤُونَ ﴿6﴾ 6

Al-Ladhīna Hum Yurā'ūna
Those who make show [of their deeds] (6)

●●●●●

وَيَمْنَعُونَ الْمَاعُونَ ﴿7﴾ 7

Wa Yamna`ūna Al-Mā`ūna
And withhold [simple] assistance. (7)

سورة الكوثر
Sourate Al-Kawthar

Bismi Allāhi Ar-Raḥmāni Ar-Raḥīmi
بِسْمِ اللهِ الرَّحْمَٰنِ الرَّحِيمِ

إِنَّا أَعْطَيْنَاكَ الْكَوْثَرَ ﴿1﴾ 1

'Innā 'A`ṭaynāka Al-Kawthara
Indeed, We have granted you, [O Muhammad],
al-Kawthar. (1)

●●●●●

فَصَلِّ لِرَبِّكَ وَانْحَرْ ﴿2﴾ 2

Faşalli Lirabbika Wa Anḥar

So pray to your Lord and sacrifice [to Him alone]. (2)

• • • •

إِنَّ شَانِئَكَ هُوَ الْأَبْتَرُ ﴿3﴾ 3

'Inna Shāni'aka Huwa Al-'Abtaru

Indeed, your enemy is the one cut off. (3)

سورة الكافرون
Sourate Al-Kafirune

Bismi Allāhi Ar-Raḥmāni Ar-Raḥīmi بِسْمِ اللهِ الرَّحْمَنِ الرَّحِيمِ

قُلْ يَا أَيُّهَا الْكَافِرُونَ ﴿1﴾ 1

Qul Yā 'Ayyuhā Al-Kāfirūna

Say, "O disbelievers,(1)

• • • • •

لَا أَعْبُدُ مَا تَعْبُدُونَ ﴿2﴾ 2

Lā 'A`budu Mā Ta`budūna

I do not worship what you worship.(2)

• • • •

وَلَا أَنتُمْ عَابِدُونَ مَا أَعْبُدُ ﴿3﴾ 3

Wa Lā 'Antum `Ābidūna Mā 'A`budu

Nor are you worshippers of what I worship.(3)

• • • •

وَلَا أَنَا عَابِدٌ مَّا عَبَدتُّمْ ﴿4﴾ 4

Wa Lā 'Anā `Ābidun Mā `Abadttum

Nor will I be a worshipper of what you worship. (4)

● ● ● ● ●

وَلَا أَنتُمْ عَابِدُونَ مَا أَعْبُدُ ﴿5﴾5

Wa Lā 'Antum `Ābidūna Mā 'A`budu

Nor will you be worshippers of what I worship.(5)

● ● ● ● ●

لَكُمْ دِينُكُمْ وَلِيَ دِينِ ﴿6﴾6

Lakum Dīnukum Wa Liya Dīni

For you is your religion, and for me is my religion." (6)

سورة النصر
Sourate An-Nasr

Bismi Allāhi Ar-Raḥmāni Ar-Raḥīmi   بِسْمِ اللهِ الرَّحْمَٰنِ الرَّحِيمِ

إِذَا جَاءَ نَصْرُ اللهِ وَالْفَتْحُ ﴿1﴾1

'Idhā Jā'a Naṣru Allāhi Wa Al-Fatḥu

When the victory of Allah has come and
the conquest,(1)

● ● ● ● ●

وَرَأَيْتَ النَّاسَ يَدْخُلُونَ فِي دِينِ اللهِ أَفْوَاجًا ﴿2﴾2

Wa Ra'ayta An-Nāsa Yadkhulūna Fī Dīni
Allāhi 'Afwājāan

And you see the people entering into the religion
of Allah in multitudes, (2)

● ● ● ● ●

فَسَبِّحْ بِحَمْدِ رَبِّكَ وَاسْتَغْفِرْهُ إِنَّهُ كَانَ تَوَّابًا ﴿3﴾ 3

Fasabbiĥ Biĥamdi Rabbika Wa Astaghfirhu
'Innahu Kāna Tawwābāan
Then exalt [Him] with praise of your Lord and ask
forgiveness of Him. Indeed, He is ever Accepting
of repentance.(3)

سورة المسد
Sourate Al-Masad

Bismi Allāhi Ar-Raĥmāni Ar-Raĥīmi   بِسْمِ اللَّهِ الرَّحْمَٰنِ الرَّحِيمِ

تَبَّتْ يَدَا أَبِي لَهَبٍ وَتَبَّ ﴿1﴾ 1

Tabbat Yadā 'Abī Lahabin Wa Tabba
May the hands of Abu Lahab be ruined,
and ruined is he.(1)

مَا أَغْنَىٰ عَنْهُ مَالُهُ وَمَا كَسَبَ ﴿2﴾ 2

Mā 'Aghná `Anhu Māluhu Wa Mā Kasaba
His wealth will not avail him or that which
he gained.(2)

سَيَصْلَىٰ نَارًا ذَاتَ لَهَبٍ ﴿3﴾ 3

Sayaşlá Nārāan Dhāta Lahabin
He will [enter to] burn in a Fire of [blazing] flame(3)

وَامْرَأَتُهُ حَمَّالَةَ الْحَطَبِ ﴿4﴾ 4

Wa Amra'atuhu Ĥammālata Al-Ĥaţabi

And his wife [as well] - the carrier of firewood. (4)

5 ﴿5﴾ فِي جِيدِهَا حَبْلٌ مِّن مَّسَدٍ

Fī Jīdihā Ĥablun Min Masadin
Around her neck is a rope of [twisted] fiber. (5)

سورة الإخلاص
Sourate Al-Ikhlas

بِسْمِ اللهِ الرّحْمَنِ الرّحِيمِ

Bismi Allāhi Ar-Raĥmāni Ar-Raĥīmi

1 ﴿1﴾ قُلْ هُوَ اللَّهُ أَحَدٌ

Qul Huwa Allāhu 'Aĥadun
Say, "He is Allah , [who is] One, (1)

2 ﴿2﴾ اللَّهُ الصَّمَدُ

Allāhu Aş-Şamadu
Allah , the Eternal Refuge. (2)

3 ﴿3﴾ لَمْ يَلِدْ وَلَمْ يُولَدْ

Lam Yalid Wa Lam Yūlad
He neither begets nor is born, (3)

4 ﴿4﴾ وَلَمْ يَكُن لَّهُ كُفُوًا أَحَدٌ

Walam Yakun Lahu Kufūan 'Aĥadun
Nor is there to Him any equivalent." (4)

Bismi Allāhi Ar-Raḥmāni Ar-Raḥīmi

بِسْمِ اللَّهِ الرَّحْمَٰنِ الرَّحِيمِ

قُلْ أَعُوذُ بِرَبِّ الْفَلَقِ ﴿1﴾ 1

Qul 'A`ūdhu Birabbi Al-Falaqi
Say, "I seek refuge in the Lord of daybreak (1)

مِن شَرِّ مَا خَلَقَ ﴿2﴾ 2

Min Sharri Mā Khalaqa
From the evil of that which He created (2)

وَمِن شَرِّ غَاسِقٍ إِذَا وَقَبَ ﴿3﴾ 3

Wa Min Sharri Ghāsiqin 'Idhā Waqaba
And from the evil of darkness when it settles (3)

وَمِن شَرِّ النَّفَّاثَاتِ فِي الْعُقَدِ ﴿4﴾ 4

Wa Min Sharri An-Naffāthāti Fī Al-`Uqadi
And from the evil of the blowers in knots (4)

وَمِن شَرِّ حَاسِدٍ إِذَا حَسَدَ ﴿5﴾ 5

Wa Min Sharri Ĥāsidin 'Idhā Ĥasada
And from the evil of an envier when he envies." (5)

بِسْمِ اللَّهِ الرَّحْمَٰنِ الرَّحِيمِ   Bismi Allāhi Ar-Raḥmāni Ar-Raḥīmi

قُلْ أَعُوذُ بِرَبِّ النَّاسِ ﴿1﴾ 1

Qul 'A`ūdhu Birabbi An-Nāsi

Say, "I seek refuge in the Lord of mankind, (1)

مَلِكِ النَّاسِ ﴿2﴾ 2

Maliki An-Nāsi

The Sovereign of mankind. (2)

إِلَٰهِ النَّاسِ ﴿3﴾ 3

Ilahi An-Nāsi

The God of mankind, (3)

مِن شَرِّ الْوَسْوَاسِ الْخَنَّاسِ ﴿4﴾ 4

Min Sharri Al-Waswāsi Al-Khannāsi

From the evil of the retreating whisperer - (4)

الَّذِي يُوَسْوِسُ فِي صُدُورِ النَّاسِ ﴿5﴾ 5

Al-Ladhī Yuwaswisu Fī Ṣudūri An-Nāsi

Who whispers [evil] into the breasts of mankind - (5)

مِنَ الْجِنَّةِ وَ النَّاسِ ﴿6﴾ 6

Mina Al-Jinnati Wa An-Nāsi

From among the jinn and mankind." (6)

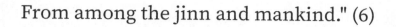

صَدَقَ اللهُ الْعَظِيمُ

"Please keep this book in a clean place
and do not throw it in the trash because
it is the word of god"

Thank you

Made in the USA
Coppell, TX
02 January 2024

27104354R10037